Habits, HURTS & Hangups

Habits, HURTS & Hangups

12 Steps to Heal the Natural Man

KEVIN HINCKLEY

CFI
An imprint of Cedar Fort, Inc.
Springville, Utah

ISBN 13: 978-1-4621-1222-7

Library of Congress Cataloging-in-Publication Data on file.

Published by CFI, an imprint of Cedar Fort, Inc.
2373 W. 700 S., Springville, UT 84663
Distributed by Cedar Fort, Inc., www.cedarfort.com

Cover design by Shawnda T. Craig
Cover design © 2013 Lyle Mortimer
Edited and typeset by Emily S. Chambers

Printed in the United States of America

10 9 8 7 6 5 4 3 2 1

Printed on acid-free paper

Other Titles by Kevin Hinckley:

Promptings or Me?

Burying Our Swords

Parenting the Strong-Willed Child

Thanks to Kimberly Wilson for her tireless help with editing, and to my wife, Cindy, for her love and support.

Contents

Introduction

Earth life, always teeming with snares and pitfalls, can leave any of us bruised, battered, and scarred. We struggle and fall and then pick ourselves back up by making necessary changes. We then attempt to get moving once again. As we do, we are painfully aware of our shortcomings—those weaknesses that shadow all our efforts to be different. To our dismay, we then repeat the same mistakes. So we start over again, hopeful that one day we'll finally summon up enough willpower to finally shed ourselves of our special brand of dysfunction that stalks us like a dark cloud in all we do.

Each time we repeat this cycle, we might be tempted to believe those small nagging thoughts—the ones that lurk around during discouragement: "Maybe this is just the way I am! Maybe I'm broken or defective! Or maybe I'm just too lazy or weak to stop doing this."

As C. S. Lewis explained, "human beings, all over the earth, have this curious idea they ought to behave in a certain way, and cannot really get rid of it. Secondly, that they do not in fact behave in that way. They know the Law of Nature; they break it. These two facts are the foundation of all clear thinking about ourselves and the universe we live in."[1]

All we know for sure is that our weaknesses remain despite our best efforts and commitments—even our whispered promises to the Lord. We know that our weaknesses rob us of happiness and often cause pain to those we love.

We have tried and continue to fail.

The good news is—and truly it is good news—that a loving Heavenly Father never intended us to perfect ourselves. It was never a part of the eternal plan of happiness. He knew that the natural man or woman within each of us, left to our own devices, would try to make this life a "self improvement" project. We would be tempted to embrace the flimsy promises of the world and, like the ancient prodigal son, eventually find ourselves lonely and empty. The natural man, wandering around in his fallen state, eventually comes to himself and discovers that he has wandered from a more exalted sphere. His inheritance is spent on things he thought would bring him happiness.

This earth experience, by its very bruising nature, can produce destructive patterns, habits, and behaviors that stunt our growth and threaten our peace. These mortal habits, hurts, and hangups act as a constant reminder. They teach that regardless of how gallant the fight, no matter how impressive the effort, we will not find the permanent change we seek *on our own.* The Lord reminds us that when we do come unto Him, "I will show unto them their weaknesses" (Ether 12:27). In fact, the closer we draw to Him, the more clearly we see those weaknesses. We then see just how much we need help beyond our frail mortal efforts.

The Savior's infinite Atonement has a twofold effect on mankind. First, it was a sinless, selfless sacrifice to redeem us from the Fall and draw all men and women unto Him. Second, the Atonement is available to help each of us daily accomplish what we cannot do on our own. His love and sacrifice can bridge the gap and lift us beyond our abilities—*if we will but allow it.* It can literally change who we are, transforming our very nature until it is brought closer to that of our creator. When that happens, we grow until we are enabled to love as He loves, serving in the same way He would.

Through the Atonement of Christ, our habits, hurts, and hangups are *taken from us*. This is not by virtue of our efforts, but often in spite of them. Accessing this marvelous power requires that we trust Him completely, looking to the power of the Atonement to change us. In short, we must completely surrender. When we do, we will then begin to do things His way and with His divine timing. He can then mold us into His image. And earthly weaknesses not part of His "Divine Nature" begin to melt away.

The following twelve steps to healing the natural man and woman follow in the tradition of Alcoholics Anonymous and the LDS Addiction Recovery Program. Seen for what they are, given the revealed knowledge of the restored gospel, these steps are literally a pathway to the transforming power of the Atonement.

Traditionally, most of us may think we have no real need for a "twelve-step" program. We calmly explain that we do not have an addiction, and that this kind of program is for someone else. All of us, however, battle the natural man and woman within. All of us have spent much of our life struggling with a variety of destructive hurts or habits that cause us and our loved ones pain. When pressed, we might even be willing to acknowledge that these habits have continued despite our best efforts to eliminate them.

This then, is a twelve-step program for healing our natural man and woman. This is a program for the rest of us!

Done individually or as a group, *Habits, Hurts, & Hangups* is designed to help walk us through the steps of divine change. A word of warning, however. Our natural man is impatient, seeking immediate results and guaranteed outcomes. The Lord, on the other hand, sees us in the broad sweep of our present struggles but also our *future* needs. With this in mind, He has His perfect timetable for us. He will remove our habits, hurts, and hangups but only when it is in our best interest to do so. Learning to trust Him also means learning to trust in His plan for our growth.

It is for this reason we begin this program of change without a clear understanding of how long it will take. If we undertake this with a goal to complete it in twelve weeks or twelve days, we will be disappointed. It will take exactly as long as it needs to take, if we will trust our Redeemer. We must let Him do it and remove all expectations of how He will do it and when.

Ready to begin?

Note

1 C. S. Lewis, *Mere Christianity* (NYC: Touchstone Books, 1996), 8.

The 12 Steps

1 Admit that you, of yourself, are powerless to overcome your habits, hurts, and hangups and that with them, your life has become unmanageable.

2 Come to believe that the power of God, through the Atonement, can heal all our ills.

3 Decide to return your will and your life to God the Eternal Father and His Son, Jesus Christ.

4 Make a searching and honest inventory of yourself.

5 Admit to yourself, to Heavenly Father, to proper priesthood authorities when necessary, and to others, those weaknesses that need to change.

6 Become entirely ready to have God remove your shortcomings.

7 Humbly ask Heavenly Father, in the name of Jesus Christ, to heal your shortcomings.

8 Make a written list of all people your weaknesses have harmed, and become willing to make restitution to them whenever possible.

9 Make a list of all people who might have harmed you and, through the Atonement of Christ, frankly forgive them.

10 Take daily personal inventory, and when you are wrong, promptly admit it and ask Heavenly Father for help.

11 Seek through humble prayer to know the Lord's will and to be empowered to carry it out.

12 Having had a spiritual awakening as a result of Jesus Christ, share the message of hope with others and practice these principles in all you do.

STEP 1

Admit that you, of yourself, are powerless to overcome your habits, hurts, and hangups and that with them, your life has become unmanageable.

For many of us, the word "powerless" causes an immediate negative reaction. Everything in modern culture teaches us that to be powerless is to be weak. To be without power is to be hurt and taken advantage of. It means being vulnerable and helpless. Society tells us we are to be strong and powerful and to take charge of our life.

For this reason, we try instead to control our life—to be in charge. To our dismay, we see our poor decision-making. We hang on to debilitating bad habits. We also notice personal weaknesses and dysfunctional habits that drain our spirituality and hurt those we love.

In our attempt to cleanse those flaws from our lives, we turn to sheer willpower and determination. We recommit and promise that things will be different—this time. We might pray more or read more scriptures, all in an attempt to quit doing painful things.

And our habits, hurts, and hangups continue to stalk our lives and rob our peace.

At some point, we are forced to finally admit that we are unable to remove these destructive elements on our own. Our weaknesses remain despite all our own efforts. Their mere presence in our lives stands as a silent testimony to our inability to take control of these shortcomings.

In truth, we cannot access the liberating power of the Atonement without first admitting—and completely believing—we are unable to change on our own. Our consistent inability to make needed changes drives us to the only real source of change, and that is the Savior. This "failure" teaches us that true healing is beyond our ability. And that He meant it to be so. Admitting we are powerless leads us to accept God's plan for us. It teaches us that we truly do need Him every hour.

In fact, the more we struggle with hurts and habits, the more clearly we are learning how powerless we really are. Of course, the first thing we must surrender is our stubborn pride—that need to be in control. Our history of repeated failures to change is a constant witness that our way does not work. It never did work!

This letting go becomes easier as we remind ourselves that the Lord loves us better than we love ourselves; that He is more interested in our eternal welfare than we are. It is His sole work and glory to bring to pass our work and glory. He intends us to live with the joy He lives with.

None of the other eleven steps will be of value to us until we first allow Him to take over the management of our private battles. There will be many times when we find ourselves struggling. When that happens, we will realize that we are again back at step one. This occurs not because we're failing, but because we're growing and need the insights gained from step one to move us forward again.

One frequently asked question is, What does surrender mean? What does it look or feel like? How do we know we're there?

We are surrendered when we discover we are more interested in God's solutions to our problems than we are in ours. We seek His loving direction—His solutions—in all we do.

We are surrendered when we spend more time listening in our prayers than telling or asking.

We are surrendered when thoughts of the Savior and the Atonement fill us with a sense of gratitude and awe.

We are surrendered when gentle counsel fills our hearts—and we follow rather than question endlessly our abilities or His motives.

We are surrendered when we embrace the idea that we are "less than the dust of the earth" and that the Savior's infinite intervention will one day bestow on us all that God has.

We are surrendered when we lose the desire to condemn others, given the amount of divine mercy extended us. We simply pray the Lord will forgive them as He has us.

We are surrendered when we cease trying to perfect ourselves and allow Him to complete us in his way and in his time.

We are surrendered when the measure of peace and hope we feel reminds us that when it is in our best interest, our habits, hurts, and hangups will be removed from us—not because of our own efforts but because of His desire for us to be whole.

We begin, then, by developing a clear recognition that we will be transformed not because we tried harder or had more willpower. We will become "as a child" (Mosiah 3:19) because we came to believe that the Savior desires to make those changes in us. He simply asks us to surrender our will to Him and let Him do it. When that happens, we are powerless but also empowered and enabled by Him.

Read and Ponder

"Now was not this exceeding joy? Behold, this is joy which none receiveth save it be the truly penitent and humble seeker of happiness." —Alma 27:18

In your life, what has prevented you from attaining the happiness you seek?

____

____

____

____

____

____

____

____

"Yea, I know that I am nothing; as to my strength I am weak; therefore I will not boast of myself, but I will boast of my God, for in his strength I can do all things." —Alma 26:12

In your "heart of hearts," how much do you trust the Lord? When do you trust Him the least?

In the past, what has happened to you when you were "weak"?

"There was given to me a thorn in the flesh, the messenger of Satan to buffet me. . . . For this thing I besought the Lord thrice, that it might depart from me. And he said unto me, My grace is sufficient for thee." —2 Corinthians 12: 7–9

What "thorns" have you been given that seem to "buffet" you the most?

Notes and Ideas

STEP 2

Come to believe that the power of God, through the Atonement, can heal all our ills.

Through step one, we came to believe we are powerless over our weaknesses. We recognized that our life becomes unmanageable when we try to live it our way. However, the Lord has never intended that we be left helpless. He desires for our life to be endowed with power—His power, from above.

The people of Alma, struggling under the load of bondage, prayed for help and deliverance from the Lamanites. Deliverance did come but not immediately. Instead, the Lord promised Alma that He would "ease the burdens which are put upon your shoulders." In response to that promise, they soon found that "the burdens which were laid upon Alma and his brethren were made light; yea, the Lord did strengthen them that they could bear up their burdens with ease, and *they did submit cheerfully and with patience to all the will of the Lord*" (Mosiah 24:14, 15; italics added).

Those who had appeared powerless over their temporary bondage gained the added strength that enabled them to do all the Lord intended them to do.

The infinite Atonement heals us in three powerful ways. First, it **Redeems**, washing away our sins in the blood of the Lamb. "Then cometh a remission of your sins by fire and by the Holy Ghost" (2 Nephi 31:17). Then the Lord declares He remembers those sins no more.

Second, the Atonement **Empowers**, helping us submit patiently until the time our burdens are removed. It was this empowering strength that enabled the people of Alma to gratefully prosper despite their bondage. They did not know how or when deliverance would come, but they bore their struggles with ease, feeling the power of God active in all they did.

Finally, the Savior's Atonement ultimately **Transforms** us, bringing about the "mighty change" of heart the Lord intends for each of us. Healing from hurts and habits is not meant to be day surgery. It is not the precise elimination of only the specific weaknesses while leaving the rest of us unchanged. It is meant to pave the way for a total transformation, becoming a new creature in Christ (2 Corinthians 5:17).

Our weaknesses cause us a great deal of pain and regret. They also impact those we love. The Prophet Alma taught that the Savior came to earth, "suffering pains and afflictions and temptations of every kind." One of the prime reasons for His earthly experience was so that He could successfully "take upon him the pains and the sicknesses of his people" (Alma 7:11).

In order to know the power of God, we need personal experiences with it. The more we recognize it working in us, the more firm our faith in Him grows and expands. As that happens, the reality of His love and His power to change becomes unmistakable.

We must come to believe He *can do it*, that He *wants to do it*, and ultimately that He *will do it*.

Given the size or amount of our weaknesses, many of us may have been led to believe that the Atonement is real for others but not for us. We may have convinced ourselves that our particular set of faults have so offended the Lord that He is unwilling to grant us the forgiveness and empowerment He extends so freely to others. We have become a special case.

As C. S. Lewis famously taught, "I willingly believe that the damned are, in one sense, successful rebels to the end; that the gates of hell are locked on the inside."[1] When we stubbornly believe He sees us differently, we keep ourselves in a hell He never intended for us to be in. Believing in His love is critical to the changes that await us.

How, then, do we come to believe that the power of God is meant for us? We must be first willing to "arouse [our] faculties, even to an experiment." This experiment begins with simply having a "desire to believe" that His love can free us from our hurts and destructive habits.

If we have this desire, Alma explains that we can "give place, that a seed may be planted in [our] heart." This seed, the love of God (1 Nephi 11:16–22), then begins to grow within us. As it does, He promises it will "begin to swell within [our] breasts," allowing us to feel its "swelling motions."

It is this swelling motion that causes us to exclaim, "It must needs be that this is a good seed, or that the [love of God] is good, *for it beginneth to . . . enlighten my understanding*, yea, it beginneth to be delicious to me" (Alma 32:28; italics added).

Allowing the Lord's love to grow within us is crucial to believing that the power of God is intended for us, despite all our ills. It is this growing knowledge that gives us hope. In time we come to fully trust that it is only by His love—the power of the Atonement—that these destructive things will be removed from our hearts and minds.

As the Prophet Mormon noted, "the preaching of the word [the love of God] had a great tendency to lead the people to do that which was just—yea, it had had more powerful effect upon the *minds of the people* than the sword, or anything else, *which had happened unto them*" (Alma 31:5).

Our habits, hurts, and hangups were planted in us from a variety of sources. Those seeds took root within us, gradually growing into the noxious trees that now torment and afflict us. Their fruit is bitter and discouraging. Unfortunately, our minds have seized hold upon the idea that these lies define who we are and what we deserve.

Yet, *each time we feel His Spirit, we directly feel His love.* And we feel it because we have given place—even for a moment—for that love within our heart. In that very instant, we should ask ourselves, "As I am feeling His love, what does that say about me—who I *really* am?" In other words, "What is my real relationship to Him and how willing is He to help me heal my weaknesses?"

The Prophet Mormon records that when the Savior came to visit the Nephites, He taught them and then prepared to leave for the evening. However, as He did so He noticed that they "did look steadfastly upon him as if they would ask him to *tarry a little longer* with them" (3 Nephi 17:5). When we are feeling His spirit and His love, we need to seize those teaching moments. "Stop and stand still" (Doctrine and Covenants 5:34), He suggested to the Joseph Smith. He is planting seeds during those times and we should avoid being in a hurry!

Finally, it is this growing understanding that gradually enlarges our soul, preparing us to have our false seeds "rooted out of [our] breast" (Alma 22:15). It helps us believe that His great power is real. And that it's not just active in the lives of those around us—it is intended for us as well.

Read and Ponder

"That they do always remember him, that they may have his Spirit to be with them. Amen."—Doctrine and Covenants 20:79

If you began to have a more constant spirit with you during the week, how would your life be different?

____

____

____

____

____

____

____

____

"The submission of one's will is really the only uniquely personal thing we have to place on God's altar. It is a hard doctrine, but it is true."—Neal A. Maxwell[2]

Is the submission of your will a "hard doctrine"? If so, what is there about this process that is so difficult?

In response to Alma's lesson on the word and the seed, the Zoramites asked "how they should plant the seed . . . or in what manner they should begin to exercise their faith" (Alma 33:1). In your own life, what will "planting the seed" look like to you?

Notes and Ideas

Notes

1 C. S. Lewis, *The Problem of Pain,* (NYC: HarperOne, 2009), 127.

2 Neal A. Maxwell, "Insights from My Life," *Ensign*, August 2000, 9.

STEP 3

Decide to return your will and your life to God the Eternal Father and His Son, Jesus Christ.

The Children of Israel faced a difficult dilemma. In response to their repeated complaints against Moses, the Lord had sent "flying fiery serpents," which poisoned most of the people. Many had already died as a result. The rest, pleading to Moses for relief, were told that they needed only to look to a brass serpent, erected on a pole. Look and they would live. Refuse and they would die.

Incredibly, even with deadly venom coursing through their veins, many refused to do even this very simple act. The reason, Alma explains, was that "they did not believe that it would heal them." He then goes on to ask: "O my brethren, if ye could be healed by merely casting about your eyes that ye might be healed, would ye not behold quickly?" (Alma 33: 20–21).

Nephi, recalling the same incident, concludes, "the labor which they had to perform was to look; and *because of the simpleness of the way*, or the easiness of it, there were many who perished" (1 Nephi 17:41; emphasis added).

In truth, most of us believe that our Heavenly Father is more knowledgeable than us, is more loving than we are, and sees our future with perfect clarity. We will also confess that following His plan results in more happiness than our plans do. And yet, despite all this, we still persist in trying to eliminate our hurts and habits our way. The result is that our lives become unmanageable.

In *Mere Christianity*, C. S. Lewis taught, "Submit to death, death of your ambitions and favorite wishes every day and death of your whole body in the end: submit with every fiber of your being, and you will find eternal life. Keep back nothing. Nothing that you have not given away will be really yours. Nothing in you that has not died will ever be raised from the dead. . . look to Christ and you will find Him, and with Him everything else thrown in."[1]

This complete submission of our will can be painful and challenging. Looking to God and allowing Him to heal "all our ills" requires that we be "stripped of pride" (Alma 5:28). It requires that we surrender cherished ideas of what it is we think we need. It also causes us to abandon past behaviors we thought would make us happy. What we begin to understand is that any other path, especially our own, delays our healing and growth.

As we submit and begin to trust Him, we will begin to find ourselves empowered by His loving care. We will feel an increasing desire, as Elder F. Enzio Busche once described, for the Lord to become "*the doer of all our deeds* and . . . the speaker of *all* our words."[2]

This desire will then produce a change in the way we pray. The primary goal of our prayers will be the "education of our desires."[3] Like a child, we will be more anxious to discover His divine perspective of our weaknesses along with His inspired direction for our healing. In our prayers, we will speak less and listen more.

We will then be more attuned to watch for "tender mercies" when they occur, recognizing them as a sought-for answer to our prayers. Seeking His guidance and counsel, we will "pour out [our] souls in [our] closets, and . . . secret places, and in [our] wilderness" (Alma 34:26).

When we are submissive in our prayers, seeking God's solutions rather than ours, needed guidance will be given. Describing just such an experience, President Henry B. Eyring relates:

> I prayed, but for hours there seemed to be no answer. Just before dawn, a feeling came over me. *More than at any time since I had been a child, I felt like one.* My heart and my mind seemed to grow very quiet. There was a peace in that inner stillness.
>
> Somewhat to my surprise, I found myself praying, "Heavenly

> Father, it doesn't matter what I want. *I don't care anymore what I want.* I only want that Thy will be done. That is all that I want. Please tell me what to do.[4]

When we are ready, becoming "submissive, meek, humble, patient, full of love, willing to submit to all things" (Mosiah 3:19), then our Heavenly Father responds with an outpouring of love and support.

But we must decide.

Many habits, hurts, and hangups come from trying to exercise our control over the painful parts of life—without success. For today, we must make a conscious decision to let go of that need to be in control and to let Him guide us where we need to be. Tomorrow we will need to make the same decision.

Like the Children of Israel, experiences with various "serpents" in our lives have left us with fatal poisons in our veins. If we do nothing, these poisons will kill us spiritually. In order to be healed, He asks only that we look to Him and live.

But we must decide.

Read and Ponder

When you visualize submitting to the Lord, what do you picture?

Read the story of Naaman in 2 Kings 5:1–14. Even though he went to great lengths to be healed, Naaman kept trying to direct how that healing would occur. What kind of things do you do, in your life, to attempt to direct or control how your growth should look?

"But behold, I, Nephi will show unto you that the tender mercies of the Lord are over all those whom he hath chosen, because of their faith, to make them mighty even unto the power of deliverance."—*1 Nephi 1:20*

The Lord's tender mercies provide constant reminders that He is aware of us and our struggles. How have His tender mercies blessed your life?

Notes and Ideas

Notes

1 C. S. Lewis, *Mere Christianity*, 225.
2 F. Enzio Busche, "Truth Is the Issue," *Ensign*, November 1993.
3 Joseph F. Smith, *Gospel Principles*, 297.
4 Henry B. Eyring, "As A Child," *Ensign*, May 2006.

STEP 4

Make a searching and honest inventory of yourself.

In the course of our lives, how often do we replay an embarrassing incident or past decision in our minds and cringe, asking ourselves, *Why did I do that?*

This leads us to the bigger question: Why do we do anything we do?

Truthfully, what we believe, about ourselves and others, determines our daily choices. Our mind retains a set of core beliefs about who we are as well as those we love. These beliefs, which drive our emotions, lie at the root of all our decisions, good and bad. Our actions are a reflection of who we think we are.

Beliefs ➡ Emotions ➡ Actions

In truth, a negative self-image often leads to poor decision-making. These destructive decisions then reinforce our negative image. One feeds upon the other and fuels our habits, hurts, and hangups.

Writing a searching and honest life story allows us to see our life in perspective—our self-images, both healthy and unhealthy, matched against our past experiences and understandings. This sweeping accounting brings to mind a treasure trove of events we may have forgotten. These memories may help us locate the genesis of negative self-images and see them in a more mature light.

In the Book of Mormon, Alma explained that the Nephites

were greatly blessed to have access to the Plates of Brass. "They have enlarged the memory of this people," he taught, "and convinced many of the error of their ways, and . . . the knowledge of their God" (Alma 37:8). The plates enabled them to realize "the great things the Lord [had] done for their fathers; and that they may know the covenants of the Lord, that they are not cast off forever" (title page of the Book of Mormon). The more they understood the truth, the more clearly they could see the breadth of the Lord's love and covenants. As a result, they understood how their creator saw them—*who they really were and not who they thought they were.*

It also showed them the history of His miracles and dealings with Israel. That added knowledge "enlarged" their memory, helping counteract false ideas taught to them by other sources. They were then able to see the truth and begin making better choices.

Taking inventory enlarges our own personal memory. We carefully detail the painful and the embarrassing, the successes as well as the follies. By doing so, we see the past through the eye of history. We then add our current understanding. This additional clarity comes as we see our childhood experiences through adult eyes rather than the limited perceptions of a child.

And inventory also allows us to understand the powerful and lasting influence of our family of origin. Family hurts and habits, perhaps extending back generations, help form a sense of who we are. We then see how *their* choices impacted *our* choices.

Most of our "core beliefs," deeply held perceptions of our abilities and self worth, form very early in life. Early childhood impressions weave themselves tightly around future choices. They strongly impact what we think we can and cannot expect from our life. They define the risks we take and the relationships we form. Taking an inventory details those early impressions, revealing the role they played in our earliest choices.

Understandably, a life's inventory can also be painful and uncomfortable. As the Prophet Moroni prepared the Nephite inventory—the Book of Mormon—he worried that future readers would mock and dismiss his writings. The Lord responded by reminding him of an eternal truth: "if men come unto me I will show unto them their weakness" (Ether 12:27). And while our inventory is probably not intended for future generations to read, it will better expose our weaknesses.

Thankfully, the Lord also reminds us that "I give unto men weakness that they may be humble: and my grace is sufficient" (Ether 12:23, 27). His love and grace will attend us as our "weak things become strong." Our inventory may also remind us of times when His tender mercies were extended to strengthen those "weak things" in our life.

In short, our lives became unmanageable due to poor choices and feeble attempts to "fix" them our way. Without the Savior's Atonement, these individual weaknesses can continue to debase our lives and impact those around us. An inspired personal inventory can help outline those weaknesses. It enables us to acknowledge the true amount of damage they've caused and fill us with a greater desire to have them removed.

Taking the time to fill out a searching and detailed inventory is an important part of the process. It helps us to prepare to have the Lord remove our weaknesses. As we fearlessly complete it, the Spirit will bring to our mind details about our lives we need to comprehend. By doing so, we will better understand the nature—and the origins—of the choices that disrupt our lives now.

Each of us will complete this inventory differently. For some, they prefer this to be a detailed history of their life. For others, this will be divided into categories. Complete it in the way you feel most inspired to do.

In addition, here are some possible tips:

- Include what you considered to be the most memorable experiences of your life: *positive and negative.* The events we recall have great significance to how we see ourselves in the present.

- Include a list of your greatest strengths as well as your weaknesses. Remember, a personal inventory is not expected to be a list of all your negative attributes and mistakes. Your life has been a combination of good and bad. Combined, they have helped form how you see yourself at present.

- You might consider the people and relationships who had a positive or negative impact on you. How we view the world is a result of all the interactions we've had with other people in our lives. Who impacted yours?

- What did you learn from your family of origin as you grew up? How did your parents deal with anger or frustration? How did they make decisions? Did you have a role in the family (oldest child, rebel, achiever, and so on)?
- The ages of eleven through fifteen are critical to the development of our self-image. Experiences and peer feedback can have a monumental effect on the developing view we have of ourselves at that age. Were you given a nickname? How did other children at school view you? Were you popular? A loner? Physically, did you develop early or late? How did teachers at the time describe you? If we were watching a video of you at that age, what would we see?

Again, taking a personal inventory, when guided by the Spirit, allows us a window into who we are and how we got here. It can serve as a reminder of all the factors and people that have contributed to our overall growth and development. Through it, we may be able to see, more clearly than ever, poor decisions we've made. But we may also be more forgiving, as we see the many factors that impacted how we see ourselves and our place in the world.

Taking a personal inventory can be uncomfortable and time-consuming. It will also be rewarding and insight-producing. It is a critical part of helping us better understand the person the Lord desires to remake.

Read and Ponder

"When you look in the dictionary for the most important word, do you know what it is? It could be 'remember.' Because all of (us) have made covenants . . . our greatest need is to remember. That is why everyone goes to sacrament meeting every Sabbath day—to take the sacrament and listen to the priests pray that (we) 'may always remember him and keep his commandments which he has given (us).' . . . 'Remember' is the word." —Spencer W. Kimball[1]

As you look back at your childhood, how can remembering past blessings help you keep the sacred covenants you've made?

____

____

____

____

____

____

____

____

"And now, behold, when I thought this, I could remember my pains no more; yea, I was harrowed up by the memory of my sins no more.
"And oh, what joy and what marvelous light I did behold; yea, my soul was filled with joy as exceeding as was my pain!" —*Alma 36:19–20*

How would your life be different if you could remember your pains "no more"?

____

____

____

____

____

____

____

____

"But behold, I, Nephi, will show unto you that the tender mercies of the Lord are over all those whom he hath chosen, because of their faith, to make them mighty even unto the power of deliverance." —*1 Nephi 1:20*

As you inventory, you begin to see moments when the Lord directed you away from potentially destructive relationships or situations. What is an example of a divine intervention you've experienced?

Notes and Ideas

Note

1 Spencer W. Kimball, "Circles of Exaltation" (address to religious educators, Brigham Young University, 28 June 1968), 8.

STEP 5

Admit to yourself, to Heavenly Father, to proper priesthood authorities when necessary, and to others, those weaknesses that need to change.

Habits, hurts, and hangups are not only destructive but also shame-producing and embarrassing. We hide them, we deny them, we downplay and ignore them. And we do all we can to keep them out of the public eye. Yet, they impact those we love and disrupt relationships all around us. In the end, we do not act out in isolation. Conversely, we also do not heal in isolation either.

From the depths of Liberty Jail, a despondent Joseph Smith wrote:

> those who have not been enclosed in the walls of prison without cause or provocation, can have but little idea how sweet the voice of a friend is; one token of friendship from any source whatever awakens and calls into action every sympathetic feeling; it brings up in an instant everything that is passed;
>
> It seizes the present with the avidity of lightning; it grasps after the future with the fierceness of a tiger; it moves the mind backward and forward, from one thing to another, until finally all enmity, malice, and hatred, and past differences, misunderstandings and mismanagements are slain victorious at the feet of hope.[1]

Can "enmity, malice, and hatred" be "slain victorious" by heeding the words of a friend? Certainly. To His disciples, the Lord declared, "ye are they whom my Father hath given me; ye are my friends" (Doctrine and Covenants 84:63). Even the Savior took solace from those He declared "friends."

After his creation, Adam "gave names to all the cattle, and to the fowl of the air . . . but as for Adam, there was not found an help meet for him" (Moses 3:20). In the Garden of Eden, the need for his own "helpmeet" became quickly apparent. Eternal progress required that Adam not be alone.

Our own growth and healing requires "helpmeets"—friends and mentors who assist us along the way. It was never intended that we do this critical work alone. This requires that we be honest and open about the true nature of our weaknesses with at least one other person. By finally revealing our weaknesses to someone else, the curtain of secrecy and shame rises on the destructive patterns that control our lives and rob us of happiness. The added perspective of a friend can aid us, stripping away false beliefs, thus diminishing the power our weaknesses have over us.

Some behaviors require disclosures to a bishop or priesthood authority. If that is the case, we should move quickly to do so. Most, however, simply require the support and feedback of a caring friend, therapist, sponsor, or family member.

Failure to seek feedback from healthy and nonjudgmental friends can have serious consequences. Our hurts and habits taint how we see ourselves and how we interact with friends and family. We then see through "a glass darkly" (1 Corinthians 13), misunderstanding the actions of others and our effect on them.

Lacking a clear perspective, we may end up with a sense of hopelessness and fear that our weaknesses will always remain. Especially when our own efforts have failed to remove them. We may then begin to see ourselves as helpless *victims*, destined to always be unhappy and struggling.

If we form a victim mentality, we immediately begin to divide people around us into two distinct groups: those we see as causing or extending our pain (perpetrators) and those we hope will rescue and protect us from being hurt (rescuers). As we do we will steer clear of those we see as perpetrators because we naturally avoid pain. We will also seek out those we see as rescuers because we continually devalue our own ability to heal. We see them as someone who can fix or solve the problem we cannot.

In reality, avoiding perpetrators, those who may cause pain, while waiting on rescuers, those who can fix the problem, keeps us perpetually weaker. It hampers our reliance on the Lord and our need to then carry out His plan for us. It also discolors our relationships while devaluing our self-image.

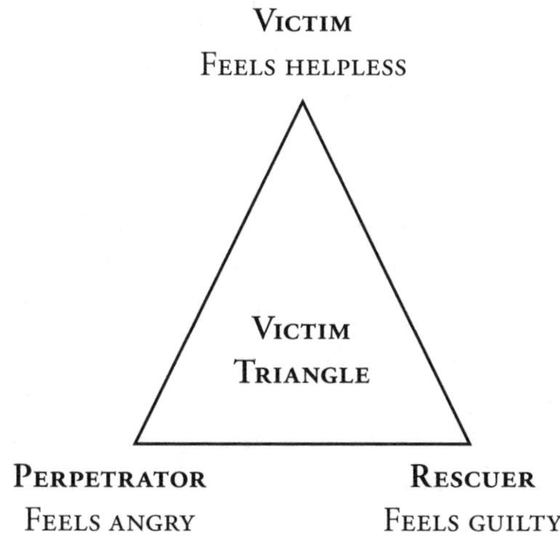

The longer we feel helpless to our hurts and habits, the longer we remain in a dysfunctional triangle. This can cause us to keep feeling—*and acting*—like a victim. Admitting to another the exact nature of our struggle begins the process of removing false understandings we have about ourselves and how others see us.

The longer we view ourselves as a victim, the more negatively it affects those who could truly help us as well. While we should seek insight from others, we need perspective not rescuing. When we are being "rescued," our present circumstance is "fixed" but our capacity to learn problem-solving skills is unchanged. Healing involves drawing on the Lord's divine counsel and accepting loving support from those around us. We then take that love and counsel and move forward.

Remember, fixing is not love, no matter how well-intentioned. It keeps the victim weaker.

Real healing changes the way we interact with others. It helps us identify those who will be supportive as we work with the Lord to make necessary changes. It also alters the way we serve others and the reasons we serve them. As we turn our will over to Heavenly Father, recognizing we are powerless, we will be filled with love and desire to help others. He plants that love deep within us. We are then more open to letting others serve us, gratefully acknowledging their help.

It also means that we carefully choose someone to be completely open with about our weaknesses. In traditional twelve-step programs this is usually a sponsor. It can be a bishop, a spouse, a friend. It can be a professional counselor or life coach. But this is someone we trust who can love us without an expectation of needing to fix us and who can give counsel when we seek it without heavy advice-giving. It is someone who can read through our personal inventory and provide added prospective.

In short, having this confidant is one more reminder that the Lord never expected this process to be done in isolation.

Read and Ponder

"And I would command you to take it upon you to counsel with your elder brothers in your undertakings; for behold . . . ye stand in need to be nourished by your brothers. And give heed to their counsel." —Alma 39:10

Whose counsel do you greatly respect? Why would you find it easy or difficult to follow their counsel?

____

____

____

____

____

"And they came to a place which was named Gethsemane; and saith to his disciples, Sit ye here while I shall pray . . .
"And he cometh, and findeth them sleeping, and saith unto Peter, Simon, sleepest thou? Couldest not thou watch one hour?" —Mark 14:32, 37

Why do you think the Savior was so anxious to have His disciples with him and awake during the suffering of the Atonement?

"My son, peace be unto thy soul; thine adversity and thine afflictions shall be but a small moment; . . .
"Thy friends do stand by thee and they shall hail thee again with warm hearts and friendly hands." —Doctrine and Covenants 121:7, 9

As you look more closely at those you consider your friends, how do you feel about approaching one of them as someone who could provide you with honest feedback about your hurts and habits?

Notes and Ideas

Note

1 Joseph Smith, *History of the Church,* vol. 3, 293.

STEP 6

Become entirely ready to have God remove your shortcomings.

In step two, we talked about giving place in our hearts that a seed may be planted within us (Alma 32:28). This seed, the love of God, then begins to grow. Just as the seeds we plant in a garden, we cannot cause this seed to grow by our own efforts nor can we dictate what kind of plant it will become. How it grows is a miracle. It is the nature of what a seed can be when nurtured in fertile soil.

Without true understanding, we attempt to change ourselves by vainly trying to remove our weaknesses on our own. In the past, we may have thought that increased willpower or more exertion removes our hurts and habits. Thus, when that effort failed, we became discouraged, blaming ourselves for not trying hard enough. We may have then concluded we are simply too weak; that we are forever destined to repeat this cycle—*endlessly*—the rest of our life.

And yet, to a group of fearing Israelites, the Lord simply declared, "Ye shall not need to fight in this battle: set yourselves, stand ye still, and see the salvation of the Lord with you, O Judah and Jerusalem: fear not, nor be dismayed; tomorrow go out against them: for the Lord will be with you" (2 Chronicles 20:17).

The Lord repeatedly declares his willingness to fight our battles, saying, "I will go before your face. I will be on your right hand and on your left, and my Spirit shall be in your hearts, and mine angels round about you, to bear you up" (Doctrine and Covenants 84:88).

The Savior intends to remove all our ills (Alma 7:11). For this reason, we must constantly remind ourselves: we do not remove them, He does. Our mortal efforts will ultimately fail, His will not. His transforming love, growing into a tree of life within us, will lift and change and transform us, if we do not "cast it out by [our] unbelief" (Alma 32:28).

The children of Israel did not know how to part the Red Sea, yet it parted. In a very similar way, we surrender our will when we finally accept that we do not know how to heal our brain of the destructive hurts and habits we've accumulated over our lifetime. We finally recognize our powerlessness when we trust that our weaknesses will be healed by the very same being who parted the Red Sea.

Elder Dallin H. Oaks explained the Lord's great intervention by saying:

> I have spoken about miracles . . . But the greatest miracle is not in such things as restoring sight to the blind, healing an illness, or even raising the dead, since all of these restorations will happen, in any event, in the resurrection.
>
> Changing bodies or protecting temples are miracles, *but an even greater miracle is a mighty change of heart by one son or daughter of God.* . . . It introduces the perspective and priorities that lead us to make the choices that qualify us for eternal life, the greatest of all the gifts of God.[1]

Here in step six, we become entirely ready to ask the Lord to do this for us. But why does this take a separate step? *Can't I just skip this step and move right to step seven?* The key to this step is the word *entirely.* This will take more emotional groundwork than we might expect.

Part of preparing is gaining a clearer understanding of what removing our weaknesses will do *to us*, not just *for us.* It will forever change us. The mighty change (Alma 5:17) alters relationships because of the way we now interact with others. It causes us to reevaluate our life plans as well as our goals. As we've discussed before, these changes will tear us from our comfort zones, propelling us to do things we've long avoided. We must be prepared not to avoid while we're being stretched and changed.

C. S. Lewis famously described this transformation:

> The terrible thing, the almost impossible thing, is to hand over your whole self—all your wishes and precautions—to Christ.
>
> Christ says "Give me All. I don't want so much of your time and so much of your money and so much of your work: *I want You.* I have not come to torment your natural self, but to kill it. No half measures are any good.
>
> I don't want to cut off a branch here and a branch there, I want to have the whole tree down. I don't want to drill the tooth, or crown it, or stop it, but to have it out. Hand over the whole natural self, all the desires which you think innocent as well as the ones you think wicked—the whole outfit. I will give you a new self instead. In fact, I will give you Myself: My own will shall become yours.[2]

Becoming entirely ready means being at peace with changing. It means coming to believe—really believe—that His plan for us is better than the myopic plans we had for us. It means letting go of our pride and truly saying, "I trust Him more than I trust me."

Over our lifetime, our habits, hurts, and hangups gave us a false image of God and His relationship with us. By looking through "a glass darkly" (1 Corinthians 13:12), we failed to understand our true needs as well as the Lord's plan of us. Thankfully, the first five steps put us in a position to challenge our false beliefs and finally get answers to these critical and soul-searching questions.

Preparing to ask God to remove our weaknesses helps us demonstrate our faith in how we will be healed. It is an open statement, trusting that our Heavenly Father really intends to heal us. It is also an act of faith, suggesting that we trust in His divine timing and in His vision for our future happiness.

Read and Ponder

"But even unto this day, when Moses is read, the veil is upon their heart. "Nevertheless when it shall turn to the Lord, the veil shall be taken away. "Now the Lord is that Spirit; and where the Spirit of the Lord is, there is liberty." —2 Corinthians 3:15–17

In what way have your weaknesses cast a veil over your heart? If the Lord removed that veil, what would you discover?

"'Spirit!' Scrooge cried, tight clutching at its robe, 'hear me! I am not the man I was. I will not be the man I would have been but for this intercourse. Why show me this, if I am past all hope?'" —Charles Dickens[3]

If your habits, hurts, and hangups were removed, what do you picture your life would be like? How would it be different than it is right now?

Notes and Ideas

Notes

1 Dallin H. Oaks, "Miracles," *Ensign*, June 2001, 6.
2 C. S. Lewis, *Mere Christianity*, 167.
3 Charles Dickens, *A Christmas Carol* (NYC: North-South Books, 2001), 4.

STEP 7

Humbly ask Heavenly Father, in the name of Jesus Christ, to heal your shortcomings.

In step six, we began to prepare ourselves for the Lord to heal us. First, we had to ask ourselves fundamental questions about our communication with our Heavenly Father. For instance: *Do I honestly believe He is anxious to answer my prayers? In my heart of hearts, do I really believe I am worthy enough to have Him heal me, despite my weaknesses?*

These are critical questions. They give us insight into whether we will allow the Lord to direct where we are to be and to follow what He'd have us do. In addition, we should also ask:

- Do I believe my Heavenly Father truly loves me?
- Does He love me as much as other people I know?
- Does He completely understand my weaknesses?
- Is He anxious to have them removed from me?
- Does He know what it will take for my weaknesses to be healed?
- Will His methods of healing be better than mine will?

If we can honestly say we believe these questions to be true—and feel ready to accept any all and changes He makes in us—then we are anxious to hear His voice, learn His will, and follow His direction.

In short, our ability to *hear and follow* becomes the most important task of our existence.

Unfortunately, past experiences with prayer may have convinced us to be wary of the answers we think we've received. We may have thought we got an answer to prayer only to follow it with disastrous results. Or we constantly sort through our own thoughts and emotions, causing us to doubt the source of the answers we do receive.

Painful hurts and habits can leave our self-esteem in tatters. We can doubt ourselves and then become overly reliant on the advice of others. These opinions—regardless of how well meaning they are—can cause us to second guess actual divine answers we've received. *If they say it, it must be true!*

Humbly asking Heavenly Father to remove our shortcomings requires learning *how* to ask and how to hear him. In this process we learn how to correctly recognize His voice and have the courage to follow it.

Remember, there is a reason that petitioning the Lord is not step one. The previous six steps have all been preparation for this request. We have learned to recognize our powerlessness. We have sharpened our understanding that the only way these changes will occur is through the Atonement of Christ. And, we have chosen to believe He is willing to make the needed changes in us.

How, then, do we ask? And what do we ask Him for? In teaching us about prayer, the Savior explained, "use not vain repetitions . . . *for your Father knoweth what things ye have need of, before ye ask him*" (Matthew 6:8). In other words, He already knows the healing we seek. He loves us and wants us to be whole. And He already has a plan for how and when that will occur. What, then, must we need to know? Like the Savior, we exclaim, "I can of mine own self do nothing (I'm powerless!); as I hear, I judge; and [God's] judgment is just; *because I seek not mine own will*, but the will of the Father which hath sent me" (John 5:30; italics added).

Humble prayer first begins with thanksgiving and gratitude, acknowledging His love and constant care for us. We count our many blessings when we acknowledge His hand in our lives. We can then cast our burdens on Him, explaining our fears and struggles along with our deep desires to be free of our hurts and destructive habits.

Next, express hope and faith. Based on our knowledge of His divine nature, we trust that He intends to remove our weaknesses and knows we are ready. For instance, *Thank you, Heavenly Father, for removing my weaknesses when it is in my best interest to do so! Thank you for all those things that thou is preparing to do.* Again, expressing gratitude for things He will do for us *in the future* demonstrates our understanding of His great love for His children.

Finally, we seek to learn the will of the Father, hungering to know what He wants us to do. There may be steps He requires, additional experiences we need to have. There may be those we need to serve—or some type of loving service we need to receive. Prayer then becomes focused on learning, and doing, His will. "Deliver me, O Lord, from mine enemies; I flee unto thee to hide me. *Teach me to do thy will; for thou art my God* . . . lead me into the land of uprightness" (Psalm 143:9–10).

The Apostle Paul sought healing from a certain weakness. Three times he petitioned heaven for relief. The Lord refused His prophet, saying only, "My grace is sufficient for thee: for my strength is made perfect in weakness." In accepting the Lord's timing, Paul responded, "Most gladly therefore will I rather glory in my infirmities, *that the power of Christ may rest upon me.* Therefore I take pleasure in infirmities" (2 Corinthians 12:9; italics added). This humble servant recognized that the healing he hoped for might take much longer than he had anticipated! Paul's quiet submission speaks volumes about the depth of his willingness to submit to the Lord's will.

Finally, President Ezra Taft Benson explained, "When you choose to follow Christ, you choose to be changed."[1] "No man," added President David O. McKay, "can sincerely resolve to apply in his daily life the teachings of Jesus of Nazareth without sensing a change in his own nature. The phrase 'born again' has a deeper significance than many people attach to it. This *changed feeling* may be indescribable, *but it is real.*"[2]

Read and Ponder

"For ye are the children of Israel, and of the seed of Abraham, and ye must needs be led out of bondage by power and with a stretched-out arm. . . .

"But I say unto you: Mine angels shall go up before you, and also my

presence, and in time ye shall possess the goodly land." —Doctrine and Covenants 103:17, 20

As you heal, you will see that His angels and His stretched-out arm lead you out of bondage. What will your "goodly land" look like to you?

"And now it came to pass that when the king had made an end of these sayings, and all the people were assembled together, they took their swords, and all the weapons which were used for the shedding of man's blood, and they did bury them deep in the earth.
"And this they did . . . vouching and covenanting with God, that rather than shed the blood of their brethren they would give up their own lives; and rather than take away from a brother they would give unto him; and rather than spend their days in idleness they would labor abundantly with their hands." — Alma 24:17–18

Conversion to the gospel brought dramatic changes to the daily lives of the Anti-Nephi-Lehies. When the Lord removes your weaknesses, how will your life be different?

"Finally, men captained by Christ will be consumed in Christ.

"Their will is swallowed up in His will (see John 5:30).

"They do always those things that please the Lord (see John 8:29).

"Not only would they die for the Lord, but more important they want to live for Him.

"Enter their homes, and the pictures on their walls, the books on their shelves, the music in the air, their words and acts reveal them as Christians.

"They stand as witnesses of God at all times, and in all things, and in all places (see Mosiah 18:9).

"They have Christ on their minds, as they look unto Him in every thought (see Doctrine and Covenants 6:36).

"They have Christ in their hearts as their affections are placed on Him forever (see Alma 37:36)." —Ezra Taft Benson[3]

In your experience, have you known someone you consider to be living "the surrendered life"? What about them do you wish you could emulate?

Notes and Ideas

Notes

1 Ezra Taft Benson, "Born of God," Conference Report, October 1985.
2 David O. McKay,
3 Ezra Taft Benson, "Born of God," Conference Report, October 1985.

STEP 8

Make a written list of all people your weaknesses have harmed, and become willing to make restitution to them whenever possible.

All men," taught Alma, "are in a state of nature . . . and in the bonds of iniquity." As a result, "they have gone contrary to the nature of God; therefore they are in a state contrary to the nature of happiness" (Alma 41:11).

Habits, hurts, and hangups can consistently place us in a state that is contrary to the nature of happiness. As we heal, this happiness is restored and returned to us. Alma explained that "the meaning of the word restoration is to bring back again evil for evil . . . good for that which is good; righteous for that which is righteous; just for that which is just" (Alma 41:13).

The Lord's infinite Atonement assures us that "ye shall have mercy restored unto you again; ye shall have justice restored unto you again; ye shall have a righteous judgment restored unto you again; and ye shall have good rewarded unto you again" (Alma 41:14).

On the other hand, our weaknesses cause us a great deal of pain. They interrupt our lives and make us miserable. They also negatively impact those around us. To others, we may be harsh or judgmental or expect them to cover up or excuse our misdeeds. We might be overly indulgent or enabling, thus causing unintended harm under a cloak of kindness.

As we heal, we see more clearly the effect our weaknesses may have had on others as we heal. And just as happiness is restored to us through the power of the Atonement, it is vital we prepare ourselves to do whatever we can to make restitution to those who might have been harmed by our behaviors.

In essence, we are to restore whatever we are capable of restoring.

We begin by making a list of all those who may have been impacted by our weaknesses. We ask Heavenly Father to open our mind and heart so that we can completely see the things we have done in the past. We do this knowing, that in all likelihood, the process will be painful and somewhat embarrassing. But we do it as we are filled with an increasing desire to clean these past actions from our lives and hearts.

Once we've created this list, we then pray to know when and how to approach them. The act of reaching out will be humbling and uncomfortable. The amount of reluctance we feel will be a good gauge of the amount of pride we retain. It also tests our willingness to do whatever is necessary to let go of any past behaviors that caused pain.

Obviously, some actions cause damage we're never able to adequately repair. Also, some efforts to express forgiveness or restitution might be rejected. To which, the Lord replies: "My grace is sufficient" (Ether 12:27). In other words, it is critical to our own healing that we are willing to restore what we can restore. His infinite Atonement is sufficient for everything else. Incredibly, He suffered for both the sinner *and* the victim. Both will ultimately find relief within the wings of His mercy.

The LDS Addiction Recovery manual suggests, "Although you may be terrified to consider it, you can become willing to meet the people on your list when the opportunity arises. You can prepare to do all you can to make amends to them. You can live by faith in the Lord, not the fear of what others might do. You can become willing in step eight to live a life guided by principles rather than by shame or fear."[1]

Again, recognizing the effects of our actions and asking for forgiveness requires the deepest levels of honesty. Feeling this growing honesty can be difficult because hurts and habits caused us to hide or obscure our weaknesses from others. Maintaining those secrets helped us avoid embarrassment and shame but it also damaged important relationships that might have brought us greater happiness. Thus, we lived in a constant state of shame, fearful that others would discover our hidden hurts and reject us. And we robbed ourselves of potential joy.

Joseph Smith taught that "the nearer we get to our heavenly Father, the more we are disposed to look with compassion on perishing souls . . . if you would have God have mercy on you, have mercy on one another."[2] Indeed, as weaknesses are removed from us, we are filled with His love. The effect of that love will be a growing desire to extend it to those around us. Specifically, we will want to begin with those we might have harmed.

Finally, a mighty change of heart alters the way we interact with others. It creates in us a more forgiving disposition as we walk the peaceable walk with the children of men (Moroni 7:4). We are less likely to judge and more inclined to offer mercy to friends as well as strangers. We become like the sons of King Mosiah, for whom "the very thoughts that any soul should endure endless torment did cause them to quake and tremble" (Mosiah 28:4).

Ultimately, our healing will fill us with a strong desire that others do not suffer because of our weaknesses. For this reason, we prepare to seek restitution with all we might have harmed.

Read and Ponder

"And they traveled throughout all the land of Zarahemla . . . zealously striving to repair all the injuries which they had done to the church, confessing their sins, and publishing all the things which they had seen."
—Mosiah 27:35

After their conversion, the Sons of Mosiah and Alma the Younger first strove to undo any damage they had caused because of their rebelliousness. How difficult a task will this be for you?

____

____

"It does not matter how small the sins are, provided that their cumulative effect is to edge the man away from the Light and out into the Nothing. Murder is no better than cards if cards can do the trick. Indeed, the safest road to Hell is the gradual one—the gentle slope, soft underfoot, without sudden turnings, without milestones, without signposts." —C. S. Lewis[3]

It might be easy to dismiss our actions as "no big deal" or to minimize our effect on others. In the past, how did you justify the negative effect your weaknesses had on those you love?

"We are repeatedly urged to use our time wisely forsaking the world and '[taking] up the cross daily' (Luke 9:23). I seem to remember [being] taught that God is serious about joy. Indeed, 'Adam fell that men might be and men are that they might have joy.' (2 Nephi 2:25). Even so, there is neither cheap joy nor cost-free discipleship." —Neal A. Maxwell[4]

Asking for forgiveness and offering restitution are both painful exercises. What do you expect to learn as you do so?

Notes and Ideas

Notes

1 "A Guide to Addiction Recovery and Healing," (SLC: The Church of Jesus Christ of Latter-day Saints, 2005), 48.

2 Joseph Smith, *History of the Church*, 5:24.

3 C. S. Lewis, *The Screwtape Letters* (NYC: HarperOne, 2009), 54.

4 Neal A. Maxwell, *C. S. Lewis: The Man and His Message*, "Insights on Discipleship," 14.

STEP 9

Make a list of all people who might have hurt you and, through the Atonement of Christ, frankly forgive them.

Alma explained that as we repent, we are delivered out of the "endless night of darkness" and that men and women become "their own judges" (Alma 41:7). When we heal, much of our pain and regret comes from things we have done *to others.* In this light, we might cringe at self-judging, fearing we may be overly harsh and judgmental about our past behaviors.

What we really desire on judgment day is more mercy and less judgment!

Yet, Alma was very clear about the criteria to be used on resurrection morning. "Therefore, my son, see that you are [1] merciful unto your brethren, [2] deal justly, [3] judge righteously, and [4] do good continually." These four actions, based largely on how we feel and act toward others, appear to constitute much of the basis for our future judgment. So how is it that we will judge ourselves? Alma explains: "and if ye do all these things then shall ye receive your reward; yea, ye shall [1] have mercy restored unto you again; [2] ye shall have justice restored unto you again; [3] ye shall have a righteous judgment restored unto you again; and [4] ye shall have good restored unto you again. For that which ye do send out shall return unto you again" (Alma 41:14, 15).

The powerful, eternal law of restoration suggests that by the power of the Atonement, *the mercy we extend to others constitutes the mercy we are judged by*; the righteous judgment we extend to those around us becomes the judgment by which we are judged. "Forgive us our debts," the Lord prayed, "as we forgive our debtors" (Matthew 6:12). We have become our own judges because the mercy and goodness we extend to others is restored back to us.

This mercy and goodness is critical because most of our hurts and habits had their start with the way others treated us in the past. Abuse, unkind comments, addictions—all can negatively impact how we view ourselves and the choices we make.

Thus, when we recall the past offenses of others toward us, we might be tempted to cry out, "it's not fair!" And we would be right. Pain and cruelty, inflicted on the innocent, is among earth-life's harshest realities.

For many of us, then, frankly forgiving those who may have hurt us might constitute the greatest challenge to our overall healing. By the same token, releasing that bitterness is just as critical to our growth. Elder Marion D. Hanks suggested, "The withholding of love [holding a grudge], is the negation of the spirit of Christ, the proof that we never knew him, that for us he lived in vain. It means that he suggested nothing in all our thoughts, that he inspired nothing in all our lives, that we were not once near enough to him to be seized with the spell of his compassion for the world."[1]

In forgiving, we follow the Master who said simply, "Judge not, and ye shall not be judged; condemn not, and ye shall not be condemned; forgive, and ye shall be forgiven" (Luke 6:37). In the plan of restoration, all things are eventually restored back to us, including our forgiveness and our mercy.

Ironically, the amount of the Savior's mercy toward us—grace—always exceeds what we deserve. The cosmic scales of justice always tip in our favor. Yet we do not complain about *this* gross "unfairness"!

In much the same way, those we forgive may not appear to merit our forgiveness. Their attitude or view of events may be unsympathetic to our pain. They might continue to be prideful or unrepentant. The simple fact is that they hurt us and we need to forgive them so that we can replace destructive bitterness with peace and gratitude. We do so, leaving justice in the hands of their Creator, frankly praying He will be merciful to them.

Fortunately, the Savior does not require that we just simply let go of deeply held hurts. His mortal experience, combined with the infinite Atonement, helps Him to "know according to the flesh *how to succor his people* according to their infirmities" (Alma 7:12; italics added). Thus, in the same way as He removes our own weaknesses, He also desires to remove the pain and anger of past hurts and injustices—if we will let Him.

It should be noted that forgiving someone is not the same as immediately trusting them once more. Prudence and wisdom suggests that the Lord does not expect that we place ourselves in a position to be hurt by others who may not have taken the necessary steps to change their lives and damaging behaviors. For instance, forgiveness never requires an abused woman to remain in close proximity to someone who continues to harm her. Similarly, it would be foolish to immediately reinvest money with someone who recently defrauded us out of our life's savings under the guise of forgiveness.

Finally, some hesitate to forgive, fearing that letting go of a grudge somehow diminishes the size or severity of the original offense. Forgiving might appear to be saying, "It's okay! What happened wasn't really that bad!" The truth is that forgiveness is not predicated on the size or severity of the pain. It does not excuse or diminish what was done. It simply places justice and mercy with a kind Heavenly Father who is better able to weigh all circumstances and factors in the balance.

Read and Ponder

"Not only does our eternal salvation depend upon our willingness and capacity to forgive wrongs committed against us. Our joy and satisfaction in this life, and our true freedom, depend upon our doing so. When Christ bade us turn the other cheek, walk the second mile, give our cloak to him who takes our coat, was it to be chiefly out of consideration for the bully, the brute, the thief? Or was it to relieve the one aggrieved of the destructive burden that resentment and anger lay upon us?" —Marion D. Hanks[2]

As you look at the events of your life, will forgiving others be a difficult task for you? If so, why?

"Verily I say unto you, notwithstanding their sins, my bowels are filled with compassion towards them. I will not utterly cast them off; and in the day of wrath I will remember mercy." —Doctrine and Covenants 101:9

If you forgive a past hurt or offense and extend mercy, what effect might that have on the events of your daily life? How would being filled "with compassion" help you with your own weaknesses?

"I am most amazed at the moment when Jesus, after staggering under His load to the crest of Calvary, said, "Father, forgive them; for they know not what they do" (Luke 23:34).

"If ever there is a moment when I indeed stand all amazed, it is this one. When I consider Him bearing the weight of all our sins and forgiving

those who would nail Him to the cross, I ask not 'How did He do it?' but 'Why did He do it?' As I examine my life against the mercifulness of His, I find how I fail to do as much as I should in following the Master." *—Jeffrey R. Holland*[3]

How does understanding the Savior's forgiveness help in your own forgiveness of others?

Notes and Ideas

Notes

1 Marion D. Hanks, "Forgiveness: The Ultimate Form of Love," *Ensign*, January 1974, 20.

2 Ibid.

3 Jeffrey R. Holland, "I Stand All Amazed," *Ensign*, August 1986.

STEP 10

Take daily personal inventory, and when you are wrong, promptly admit it and ask Heavenly Father for help.

In the previous steps, we learned to surrender our wills and trust in the guidance of a loving Heavenly Father. We made a personal searching inventory and admitted to ourselves and others those weaknesses that need to be changed. With that clearer understanding we humbly asked Heavenly Father to remove, in His divine timing, weaknesses and hurts we do not possess the ability to remove on our own.

We also began the process of forgiving those who might have hurt us, thus playing a part in forming our hurts and habits. Turning to the Atonement of Christ, we pled that bitterness and anger be removed from our hearts. We recognized that we'd received the gift of mercy, forgiving us for our past actions. We then began seeking the Lord's love in forgiving those who may have hurt us.

These previous steps began to enable us to "[obtain] a sufficient hope" whereby we can "enter into the rest of the Lord, from this time henceforth" (Moroni 7:3). This hope increases as we watch our destructive weaknesses diminish in power and influence. As a result, we strive even more to walk the "peaceable walk with the children of men" (Moroni 7:4).

However, this new life, as it is being stripped and cleansed of destructive habits, requires constant vigilance as we move forward. Our weaknesses often defined us, dictating who we thought we were.

They dominated our daily thoughts and impacted our decision-making. Therefore, a future life without them seems less predictable and certain. Without that certainty, we may be tempted to return to the destructive but familiar habits we've asked the Lord to remove.

It is for these reasons that we need to take a constant inventory of our daily walk as new creatures in Christ. This ongoing evaluation helps make sure we continue to progress. It also helps us address additional areas of change.

How do we do that?

To begin with, the Prophet Joseph Smith once counseled the Twelve Apostles to "make yourselves acquainted with those men who like Daniel pray three times a day toward the House of the Lord."[1] Indeed, Hebrew tradition requires the observant to offer prayers at *shaharit*, "morning light," *mincha*, or afternoon prayers, and *arvit*, "nightfall."

Most twelve-step programs rely heavily on the *morning devotional* as a key to preventing relapse. This brief few minutes of reading and prayer, first thing each morning, constitutes a solid beginning to each day. It focuses the mind and heart on the day before us. It also sets a daily determination to remain teachable and humble throughout that day.

As Alma explained:

> For behold, it is as easy to give heed to the word of Christ, which will point to you a straight course to eternal bliss, as it was for our fathers to give heed to [the Liahona], which would point unto them a straight course to the promised land.
>
> And now I say, is there not a type in this thing? For just as surely as this director did bring our fathers, by following its course, to the promised land, shall the words of Christ, if we follow their course, carry us beyond this vale of sorrow into a far better land of promise. (Alma 37:44–45)

The morning devotional acts as our personal Liahona, giving us guidance and direction for our day's journey. It thus helps to lead "the man of Christ in a strait and narrow course across that everlasting gulf of misery which is prepared to engulf the wicked—and land their souls . . . at the right hand of God" (Helaman 3:29, 30).

Daily prayer also provides us with an opportunity to constantly evaluate our behaviors and actions. It gives us a daily opportunity to seek out His will. If we will spend more time listening, it allows Heavenly Father to teach and strengthen us by the gentle promptings of the Holy Ghost. We are then filled, each day, with His love and peace. This daily divine contact helps us build a desire to remain "humble and . . . submissive and gentle, easy to be entreated; full of patience and long-suffering; being temperate in all things" (Alma 7:23).

Because we are anxious to remain submissive to His will, we know we will make mistakes in the future. The Holy Ghost can quickly prompt us to action if we are listening and teachable. Those promptings will then help us recognize weaknesses that require repentance or change. They will spur us on to recommitment and renewed determination. The Prophet Mormon explained that "as oft as they repented and sought forgiveness, with real intent, they were forgiven" (Moroni 6:8).

In addition to personal prayer, daily searching of the scriptures opens the heart and invites the Spirit. In speaking of the scriptures, the Lord has declared,

"Behold, I am God and have spoken it; these commandments are of me, *and were given unto my servants in their weakness* . . . that they might come to understanding . . . .

"And *inasmuch as they sought wisdom* they might be instructed;

"And inasmuch as they were humble *they might be made strong,* and blessed from on high, and receive knowledge from time to time." (Doctrine and Covenants 1:24–28; italics added)

Given in our weakness, His words help us better understand him. They also fill us with wisdom and strength.

Taking daily inventory is essential to our healing and growth. It requires a consistent assessment of our lives and behaviors. It also places us in a position for the Lord to continue to change us, strengthen us, and move us forward.

Read and Ponder

"The nearer man approaches perfection, the clearer are his views, and the greater his enjoyments, till he has overcome the evils of his life and lost every desire for sin" —Joseph Smith[2]

If you began taking a daily inventory of your life, in what ways would your views of your daily actions be clearer?

"If ye do not watch yourselves, and your thoughts, and your words, and your deeds, and observe the commandments of God, and continue in the faith of what you have heard concerning your Lord, even unto the end of your lives, ye must perish. And now, O man, remember, and perish not." —*Mosiah 4:30*

What daily steps or behaviors are most critical to keeping you on the straight and narrow path? What are some of your warning behaviors—actions that suggest you might be succumbing to weaknesses and destructive habits?

"As we persist, we will feel the need for the influence of the Holy Ghost because our task will seem beyond us. Our humble prayer to our Heavenly Father will be answered. The Holy Ghost has as a major purpose

witnessing that Jesus is the Christ. As we plead for help in His service, the Holy Ghost will come and confirm our faith in Him. Our faith in the Savior will increase. And, as we continue to serve Him, we will come to love Him. To be called to serve is a call to come to love the Master we serve. It is a call to have our natures changed." —Henry B. Eyring[3]

What role will service play in your "peaceable walk with the children of men"?

Notes and Ideas

Notes

1 Joseph Smith, *History of the Church,* 3:391.

2 *Teachings of the Prophet Joseph Smith*, 51.

3 Henry B. Eyring, "As a Child," *Liahona*, May 2006.

STEP 11

Seek through humble prayer to know the Lord's will and to be empowered to carry it out.

In order to better prepare the early Saints for the blessings of the temple, the Prophet Joseph Smith convened the School of the Prophets. In this school, he taught "that three things are necessary in order that any rational and intelligent being may exercise faith in God unto life and salvation. First, the idea that he actually exists. Secondly, a correct idea of his character, perfections and attributes."[1]

As we work through the healing steps, we come to a greater understanding of our Heavenly Father and His Son, Jesus Christ. We better understand their character and have a greater appreciation for their loving, healing attributes. This growing knowledge fills us with the hope necessary to move forward and trust that He will remove our weaknesses as He has promised.

Joseph Smith then explains that the third element of faith, necessary for salvation, is "an actual knowledge that the course of life that he is pursuing is according to his will."[2] In other words, for faith to be complete, we need his divine reassurance that we are daily on the path he desires for us.

Striving to know His will requires that we listen and recognize His voice when it speaks to us. In the Book of Mormon, one group described this voice by saying "that it was not a voice of thunder, neither was it a voice of a great tumultuous noise, but behold, it was a still voice of perfect mildness, as if it had been a whisper, and it did pierce even to the very soul" (Helaman 5:30).

When we surrender and allow our habits, hurts, and hangups to be healed by the Atonement, we hear His voice. We hear His voice in the peace that replaces the confusion that always accompanied our weaknesses. We hear His voice in the quiet urging to move forward in our lives.

And we hear Him directing us in the changes we now need to make in our daily actions.

We have discovered that healing is often uncomfortable, even painful. However, moving forward without the familiarity of our former habits and hangups may seem daunting—even impossible. The course corrections He is now making to our life may make little sense or be contrary to what we would have done.

Remember, in the past, each day we made choices based on our limited view of what we were capable. Now, we will be making decisions based on His loving vision of who we are to become. "Joy," offered C. S. Lewis, "is the serious business of heaven!"[3]

To those now willing to follow Him, the Savior gives a simple invitation. "Take my yoke upon you, and learn of me; for I am meek and lowly in heart; and ye shall find rest unto your souls. For my yoke is easy, and my burden is light" (Matthew 11:29, 30).

The image of the yoke, the ancient symbol of bondage, suggests that we have been "captured" by him. "Ye were not redeemed with corruptible things . . . but with the precious blood of Christ" (1 Peter 1:18). And yet, if we are to be healed of our weaknesses, we are also being called on to take upon us the yoke He carries—feeding His sheep. We are to love and serve just as He would.

How can this be? We wonder. We have lived our lives, to this point, with the cozy companionship of these destructive but familiar hurts and habits. *How will I know what to do or how to respond to challenges in life without them?*

The answer, of course, is that the Savior will empower us to do the things we are asked to do. "I will go before you face," he promises. "I will be on your right hand and on your left, and my spirit shall be in your hearts, and my angels round about you, to bear you up" (Doctrine and Covenants 84:88).

It is for this reason that we need not be dismayed by the size of the task of changing our life. He never intended us to do it alone.

To the Children of Israel, the Lord offered this reassurance: "Be not afraid nor dismayed by reason of this great multitude; for the battle is not yours, but God's" (2 Chronicles 20:15).

Before us lies a great multitude of challenges—new ways of approaching life and relationships. But, the battle is not ours alone. He will not leave us "comfortless." In moments of challenge, if we are listening, we will know what He wants us to do. As we desire to learn His will for our lives, He will direct us toward the experiences that are in our best interest and of those we are to serve.

At the same time, by virtue of our surrender and transformation, He can more fully empower us, guiding us with His spirit and helping us know how we are to accomplish all that He now asks of us.

"Be thou humble," He counsels, "and the Lord thy God shall lead thee by the hand and give thee answer to thy prayers" (Doctrine and Covenants 112:10).

Read and Ponder

"The Lord will not only magnify the power of your efforts. He will work with you Himself. His voice to four missionaries, called through the Prophet Joseph Smith to a difficult task, gives courage to everyone He calls in His kingdom: 'And I myself will go with them and be in their midst; and I am their advocate with the Father, and nothing shall prevail against them (Doctrine and Covenants 32:3).'"—Henry B. Eyring[4]

If He magnifies your efforts, how will you be different? In what way will your behaviors change?

____

____

____

____

____

____

____

____

"Seek not to counsel the Lord, but to take counsel from his hand. For behold, ye yourselves know that he counseleth in wisdom, and in justice, and in great mercy, over all his works."—Jacob 4:10

When you honestly evaluate your prayers, how much time do you spend "counseling" the Lord on the things you want him to do and how much of the time is spent trying to discover what He wants you to do? What do you need to do differently to allow Him to counsel you more often?

"Sometimes you may feel to complain to the Lord about a challenge that has come into your life through no fault of your own. . . . God knows what is best for us. Although we may not understand why we experience some things now, in His timetable we will know and be grateful." —Richard G. Scott[5]

How can complaining about our challenges prevent Him from empowering us?

Notes and Ideas

Notes

1 *Lectures on Faith*, Lecture Third (American Fork, UT: Covenant, 2000), 1.
2 Ibid.
3 C. S. Lewis, *Letters to Malcolm: Chiefly on Prayer* (Boston: Mariner Books, 2002), 92–93.
4 Henry B. Eyring, "Rise to Your Call," *Liahona*, November 2002.
5 Richard G. Scott, "He Lives," *Ensign*, November 1999.

STEP 12

Having had a spiritual awakening as a result of Jesus Christ, share the message of hope with others and practice these principles in all you do.

"Pain is not only immediately recognizable evil, but evil impossible to ignore. Pain insists upon being attended to," suggested C. S. Lewis. "God whispers to us in our pleasures, speaks in our conscience, but shouts in our pain; *it is His megaphone to rouse a deaf world.*"[1]

At some point, we determined that our habits, hurts, and hangups had caused us enough pain. We also had to admit that our approach was not working. We then began searching for a way for them to be healed. That search led us to this program. By the time we reach step twelve, we will have been engaged in a long concerted effort to find more joy while reducing the pain.

When we recognize that the healing process has truly begun, we begin to live with greater gratitude. Like Nephi, we might be led to exclaim, "He hath filled me with his love . . . behold, he hath heard my cry by day . . . yea, my voice have I sent up on high; and angels came down and ministered unto me" (2 Nephi 4:21–24). We are then willing to testify that "the tender mercies of the Lord are over all those whom he hath chosen . . . to make them mighty even unto the power of deliverance" (1 Nephi 1:20).

This gratitude and knowledge leads us to naturally reach out to those around us. When the Savior asked Peter, "Simon, son of Jonas, lovest thou me?" he responded with "yea, Lord, thou knowest that I love thee" (John 21:15). Like Peter, our new growth leads us to love, even more deeply. It comes from the Savior who has given us great gifts of healing.

It is to us, then, along with Simon Peter, that the Lord requests, "Feed my lambs."

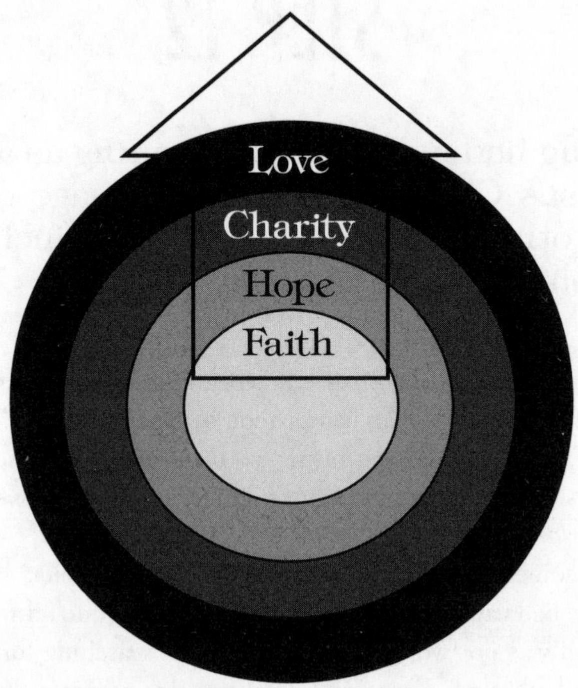

This is the reason, when discovering that "there was greater happiness and peace and rest for [us]" (Abraham 1:2), that we begin to reach out to others still struggling. Our growth is not complete if we are not active in telling His "lambs" the good news of the gospel.

To Joseph Smith Sr., the Lord explained, "And faith, hope, charity and love, with an eye single to the glory of God, qualify him for the work" (Doctrine and Covenants 4:5). These four traits, all gifts of God, build upon one another.

The removal of our destructive hurts and habits begins with a growing faith in a Heavenly Father, one who is determined to mold us into the image of His Son. Learning of Him and trusting that we are His "work and His glory" (Moses 1:39).

That faith leads to a hope that He will change us, that our lives will finally be free from painful weaknesses. That hope energizes us, enabling us to move through the uncomfortable behavioral changes that will make us whole.

As we change, gratitude grows. He is doing for us what we were unable to do for ourselves. The more grateful we feel, the more we are infused with His love; not just for us, but for all His children. Seeing others as He sees them helps us not to judge as well as to forgive. This in turn strengthens relationships around us, increasing support for us as "new creatures."

Finally, filled with this charity, we naturally reach out to those around us. We are more sensitive to others and their weaknesses. Even more important, we are learning how to love rather than to merely rescue or fix others, as we learned in step three.

We will rely on the Lord, through the quiet promptings of the Holy Ghost, to tell us when and how to reach out to those around us. We will want to share our experiences *within the Lord's divine timing,* knowing that only He understands that moment when a person in pain is ready to listen and to act.

Conversely, His inspired counsel will also alert us to those times when we are to refrain from intervening or sharing with an individual. This restraint might be because our intervention could take from them a struggle critical to their growth. We learn that *not acting* is sometimes more difficult than *doing something* to help!

Sharing the message of hope is a natural extension of the mighty change. Our experience can help others learn that their weaknesses can become strengths. We stand as a witness of the power inherent in complete surrender and reliance on the Lord of Hosts. Because this approach—the Lord's plan for our growth—is in direct opposition to our natural man's instincts, the example of a grateful survivor may give them the courage to start their own process.

We will also discover that sharing our experience with others also solidifies the steps in our own minds and hearts. We understand the journey better as we explain and teach it to those waiting to start.

So, the task is before us! Feed His lambs!

Read and Ponder

"There are so many times when genuine human service means giving graciously our little grain of sand, placing it reverently to build the beach of brotherhood. We get no receipt, and our little grain of sand carries no brand; its identity is lost, except to the Lord."—Neal A. Maxwell[2]

Who's grains of sand played a role in helping change your life? What was it they did that made the difference for you?

"Those of us who have partaken of the Atonement are under obligation to bear faithful testimony of our Lord and Savior." —Howard W. Hunter[3]

Do those around you know of your testimony of the Atonement? If not, what is it that is holding you back from sharing it?

"Yea, I know that I am nothing; as to my strength I am weak; therefore I will not boast of myself, but I will boast of my God, for in his strength I can do all things; yea, behold, many mighty miracles we have wrought in this land, for which we will praise his name forever.
"Behold, how many thousands of our brethren has he loosed from the pains of hell; and they are brought to sing redeeming love, and this because of the power of his word which is in us, therefore have we not great reason to rejoice?"—Alma 26:12–13

If you knew you were being empowered to share what you now know, how would that change who you talk to? Who would you want to talk to?

Notes and Ideas

Notes

1 C. S. Lewis, *The Problem of Pain*, 91. Italics added.

2 Neal A. Maxwell, "All These Things Shall Give Thee Experience" (SLC: Deseret Book, 2007), 63.

3 Howard W. Hunter, "The Atonement and Missionary Work," seminar for new mission presidents, June 21, 1994, 2.

Conclusion

The Gospel of Mark contains one of the great moments in the Savior's ministry. He is approached by one of the rulers of the local synagogue, Jarius. His daughter is deathly ill, and he pleads with the Savior to "lay thy hands on her," believing that "she will live" (Mark 5:23). Jesus then agrees to go with him.

However, there is another healing need also close by. One much less heralded and public. Mark explains that there is a "certain woman, which had an issue of blood twelve years, and had suffered many things of many physicians, and had spent all that she had, and was *nothing bettered, but rather grew worse*" (Mark 5:26; italics added).

Her plight is the very essence of being powerless. She has done all she knew to do. She has exhausted her resources, and, after twelve years, she is worse. Nothing has worked. Worse yet, this illness had left her at the very bottom of Jewish society. The issue of blood would have left her unclean and undesirable. She would have been unwelcome in the synagogue or anywhere in society. She might as well have had leprosy for the effect this malady had on her.

Yet, for her, there is some measure of hope. She has heard a rumor that some are being healed simply by touching the hem of the garment of this particular rabbi from Nazareth. Having tried all else, she then places herself in the narrow streets of the city and turns to the only source of healing now open to her. "If I may touch but his clothes, I shall be whole" (Mark 5:28).

Her humility is evident. She does not appear to feel worthy enough to ask him, as did Jarius. She is not on his societal level. She sees her only hope in reaching out subtly, quietly. But, there is great faith in her, as the Savior will soon attest. Healing is possible, more than she knows.

Finally the moment of desperation comes. Jesus, walking with His disciples and Jarius, passes by. She carefully reaches out, touches the Savior's hem, and then immediately retreats back into the crowd.

And it worked! The issue of blood that has plagued her for twelve long years dries up immediately. "And she felt *in her body* that she was healed." Quietly, out of the sight of the pressing crowd, a sweet and loving miracle has taken place to one of the least of society!

But her moment of joy is quickly mingled with fearing and trembling. Jesus is also aware that healing has happened. He feels "in himself that virtue had gone out of him." The word "virtue"—in Greek, *dynamis*—means inherent power. Her healing had drawn on his power. It had cost Him personally, and He could feel it.

The woman with an issue of blood had a serious physical illness she was unable to heal. But she also had a second, more potent disease that also needed the Master's attention. Her view of herself, of her social standing, of her personal worthiness was also in need of repair. Years of failure and rejection would have surely taken its toll. Her first problem, the issue of blood, had been healed. It was this second illness, however, that Jesus now addressed.

"Who touched my clothes?" He calls out, "and he looked round to see her that had done this thing."

Though she had been the recipient of a life-changing miracle, still the woman was fearful she had done something wrong. Trembling, she "came and fell down before him, and told him all the truth" (verse 33). Her response makes it clear that her second illness—her self-doubt—needed to also be healed.

With Jarius and those on the busy street watching on, the Savior issued a declaration intended for all who would hear. "Daughter, thy faith hath made thee whole; go in peace and be whole of thy plague." He wanted her to understand that the healing had come as a result of her faith and reaching out to him. His virtue had made her complete once more, but it was her desire and belief that had made that a possibility.

And so it is with each of us.

Our journey through mortality has left us with earth stains—habits, hurts, and hangups. Those weaknesses inflict us and rob us of peace and joy. Vainly we try to rid ourselves of them. Like the woman, we try a variety of things to change and heal. Yet, in the end, nothing is better. In fact, things are often worse.

At some point, we try again, completely convinced that sheer willpower and determination will work. We double on prayer and scripture study. Harder we try. And more painfully we fail. We also add guilt to the failure. If I were just more faithful, less lazy, and so on.

Somewhere, in the heavens, a loving father must watch our endless folly—smiling at our determination, but anxious to help ease our burdens. Calling out to us, then waiting for us to finally turn and accept His help. That help has always been there. It will always be more powerfully healing than all our puny efforts. All we have to do is to reach out for the hem of His garment. It's all we ever had to do.

For the children of Israel, they simply had to look to the brazen serpent and live. For the family of Lehi, they just needed to be obedient and follow the pointers on the Liahona. For powerful Naaman, he needed only to heed a prophet's voice and bathe seven times.

Over and over, through scripture, we are taught the simple lesson—look and you will live. Stubbornly, we may fail to heed that lesson, often until we are bruised and scarred with the many wounds of our own efforts.

The natural man and woman stands like an obstinate, tired toddler: refusing to budge and too miserable to stay. Eventually he or she must yield and let go.

These twelve steps provide a blueprint for letting go. They give us increased access to the saving Atonement of Christ by helping us surrender our pride along with our need to be in charge. They place us on a path toward the mighty change of heart and give us hope.

And when that happens, we will be surprised by the amount of joy He intends for us!

Notes and Ideas

ABOUT THE AUTHOR

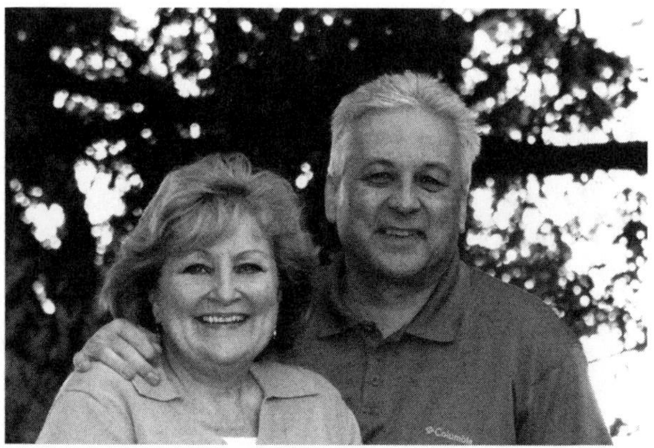

Returning author Kevin Hinckley is a licensed professional counselor in private practice. He received his master's degree in counseling from Brigham Young University, with an emphasis in organizational behavior. He has developed numerous therapeutic programs, including inpatient and day treatment programs for addiction and trauma recovery. He has worked closely with the LDS Addiction Recovery Program and is the creator of The Naaman Project, a day treatment program for pornography addiction. A former bishop and institute teacher, Kevin has written three books, *Promptings or Me?*, *Parenting the Strong-Willed Child*, and *Burying Our Swords*. He is a regular presenter at Campus Education Weeks at BYU–Idaho and BYU.

0 26575 12227 5